MY FIRST
Karate Class

By Alyssa Satin Capucilli

Photographs by Leyah Jensen

Ready-to-Read

Simon Spotlight

New York   London   Toronto   Sydney   New Delhi

This book was previously published with slightly different text and art.

For young karate enthusiasts . . . everywhere!

—A.S.C.

To Mikkel, my brother, who was every bit

worth the wait.

—L.J.

SIMON SPOTLIGHT
An imprint of Simon & Schuster Children's Publishing Division
1230 Avenue of the Americas, New York, New York 10020
This Simon Spotlight edition December 2016
Text copyright © 2012 by Alyssa Satin Capucilli
Photographs and illustrations copyright © 2012 by Simon & Schuster, Inc.
For information about special discounts for bulk purchases, please contact Simon & Schuster Special Sales at
1-866-506-1949 or business@simonandschuster.com.
Manufactured in the United States of America 1116 LAK
2 4 6 8 10 9 7 5 3 1
This book has been cataloged with the Library of Congress.
ISBN 978-1-4814-7932-5 (hc)
ISBN 978-1-4814-7931-8 (pbk)
ISBN 978-1-4814-7933-2 (eBook)
This book was previously published with slightly different text and art.

It is my first day
of karate.

My outfit is great to me!

I have a white belt.

It means I am new.

My uniform is called a gi!

First we take a breath.

Then we make a deep bow
and get our bodies ready.

We stretch and bend
and balance like a crane.

We practice big too!

Look at me!

I can stand very steady!

These are called katas in karate class.

We practice

a block, and

It is fun to learn
something new!

We prowl like tigers
and slither like snakes.

"Hai ya!"

we say with a cheer.

After one final bow,
it is time for a drink.

I am as thirsty
as a bear!

I will practice my karate every day!

Do you want to be a karate master?

Find a grown-up to help you learn the

karate moves in this book!

1
Take a Bow

Let's warm up for karate!
Stand with your feet pointing
straight ahead like two train tracks.
Bend forward at the waist to bow.

2 Stretch

Lift your shoulders up and down . . .

and up and down

and up and down again.

That feels great!

3 Bend

Now bend your body
from side to side.
Reach with your arms
and imagine you are
painting a big rainbow.

4 Balance

Stand on one leg with
your fists to the side.
Pretend you are a statue.
Try not to wobble!

Now try the other leg!
You will need this move
again and again in karate class!

1
Prowl like a Tiger!

Kneel on all fours.
Can you straighten
both legs with
a powerful roar and
push up?

2 Say "Hai ya"!

"Hai ya" is a great big "YES!" in Japanese.

Haiiiiiiiii

YAAA!

Say it when you do a movement that is just right.

3
Slither Like a Snake

How fast can you scramble on your belly?

Remember, snakes have no hands or feet to help them.

4 Drink Water

Always have a cool
drink of water when
you practice karate.
Yummy!

Practice Makes Perfect

1 Karate Belts

A karate belt is called an obi.
A white obi is for beginners.
There are other colors too,
like yellow, green, blue, and brown.
A black belt means you are an
expert in karate.

2 Slow and Steady

Slowly practice your stance,
block, punch, and kick.
It is important to do it just right.

3
Show Your Karate Moves

You can show your sensei and your friends
how well you are doing your moves.

You may even get
a new belt.
It's exciting!

4
Have Fun!

No matter what color belt you wear, enjoy yourself.

Karate is fun!